What Is Respect?

Giving Respect

Manuel Martinez

SOCIAL AND EMOTIONAL LEARNING FOR THE REAL WORLD™

Rosen Classroom™

Respect is being friendly.

Respect is being fair.

Respect is using manners.

Respect is taking turns.

Respect is listening.